Your Nose

Written by Nick Arnold
Illustrated by Maurizio De Angelis

A nose can be big. A nose can be small.
Your nose is hard on top and soft at the end.
It hurts when you bang your nose.

Your nose has two nostrils. There are hairs in the nostrils and they are wet inside.
You have snot in your nose.

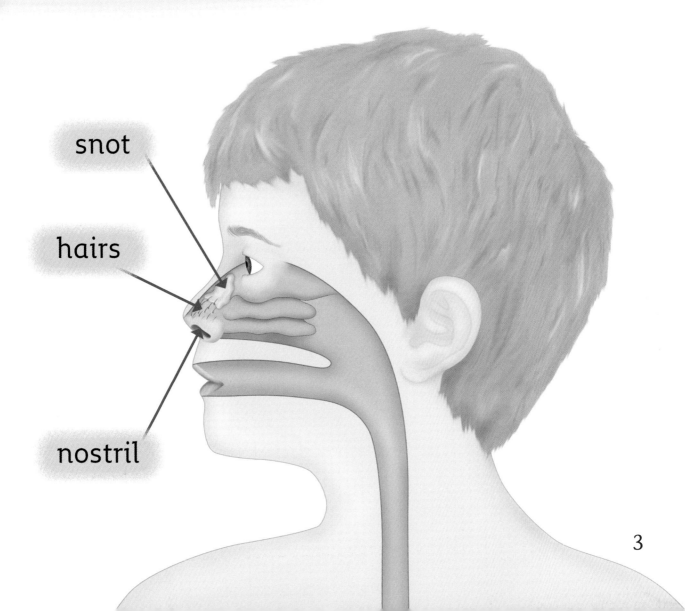

snot

hairs

nostril

Your body needs air. Your lungs suck air into your nose. Your nose heats the air on its way to your lungs.

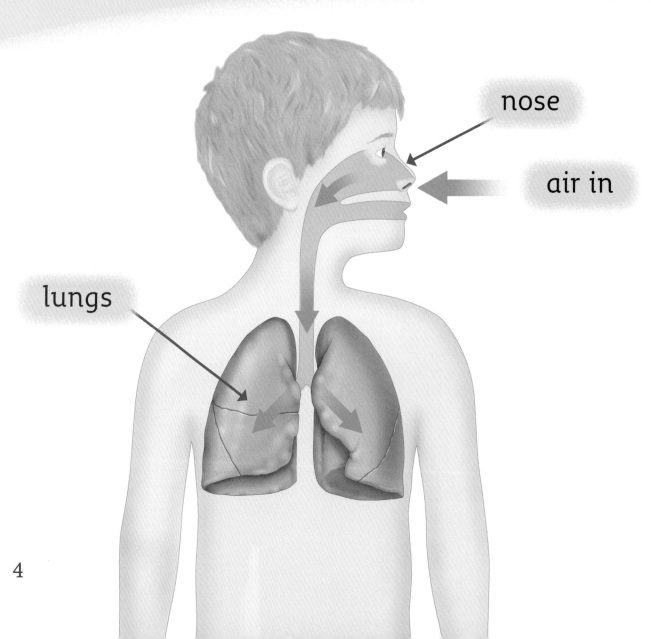

nose

air in

lungs

The air your body does not need gets blown out from your nose and mouth.

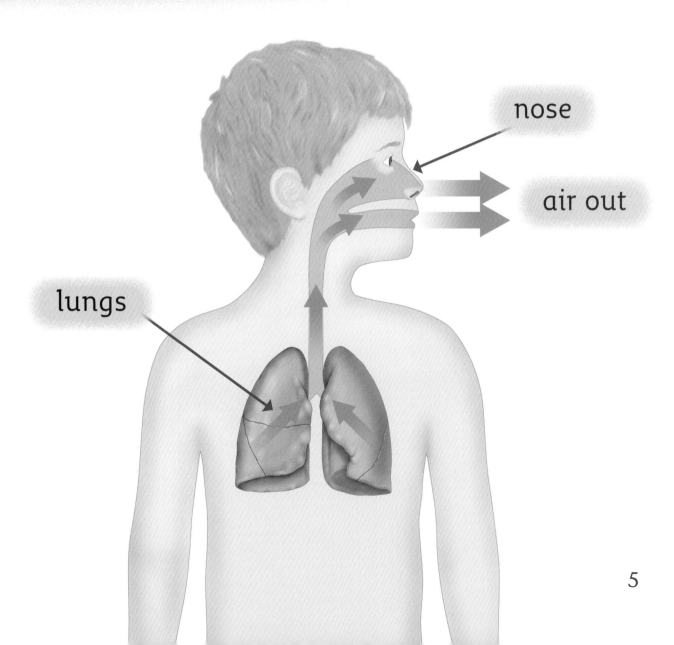

nose

air out

lungs

Your nose lets you smell. You sniff the air. The smell goes in your nostrils and up inside your head.

Inside your head the smell sets off a signal.
The signal tells your brain what the smell is.

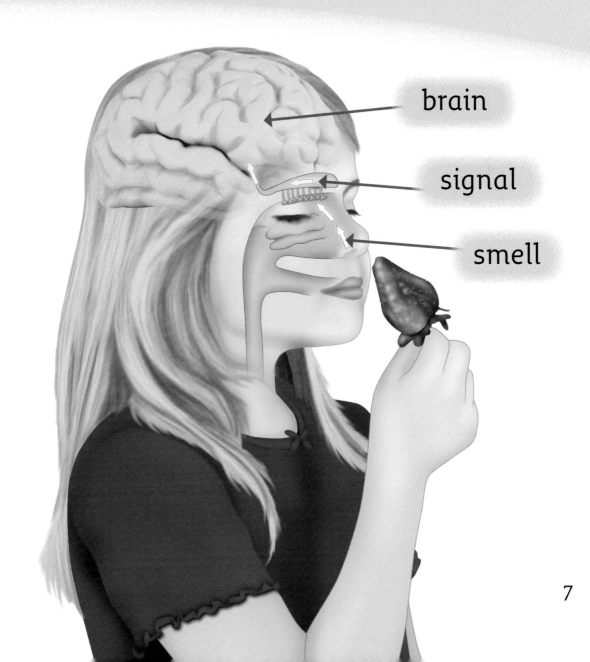

brain

signal

smell

Your nose helps you to stay safe. Smells tell
you if there is a risk. The smell of smoke or gas
can mean it is not safe.

If food smells good you want to eat it. If food is not good it smells bad. The bad smell tells you that the food can make you sick.

Your nose helps to keep dirt out of your lungs. If dirt gets in your nostrils it sticks to the snot and does not go into your lungs.

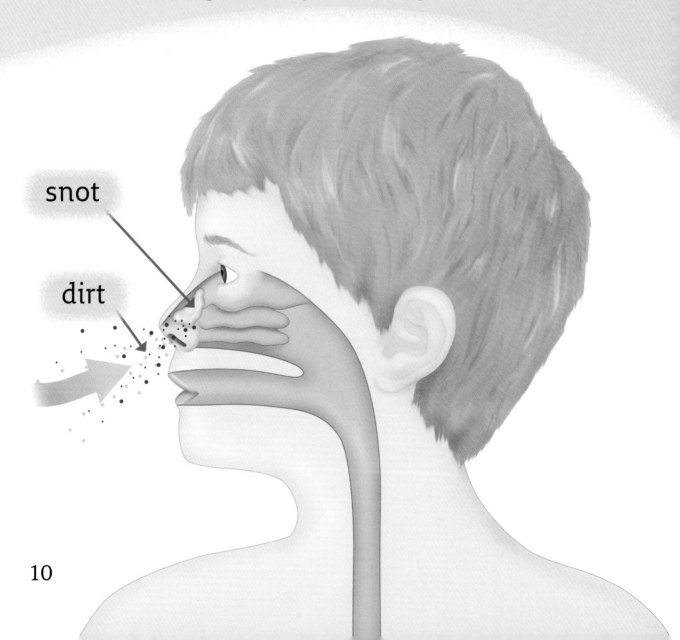

snot

dirt

Dirt and dust in your nose make you sneeze. When you sneeze, dirt and dust and snot fly out of your nose very fast.

When you are ill your
nose makes lots of snot.
You need to blow
your nose a lot.

Your nose helps you all the time. It helps you to get air, smell, keep out dirt and get better when you are ill.

Your nose

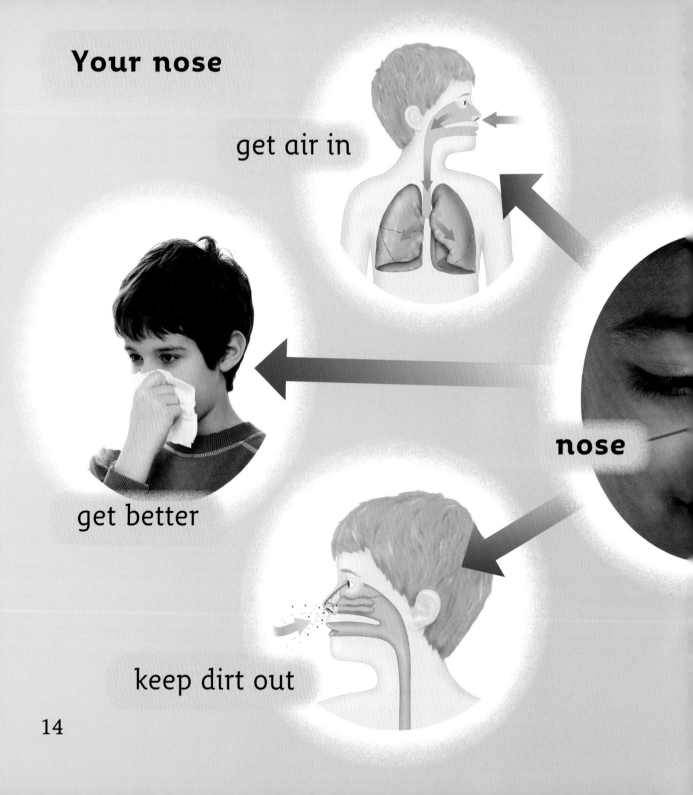

get air in

nose

get better

keep dirt out

14

smell

stay safe

tell if food is bad

15

Ideas for reading

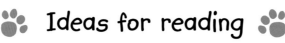

Written by Clare Dowdall BA(Ed), MA(Ed)
Lecturer and Primary Literacy Consultant

Learning objectives: apply phonic knowledge and skills as the prime approach to reading unfamiliar words; read phonically decodable two-syllable and three-syllable words; read more challenging texts which can be decoded using their acquired phonic knowledge and skills, along with automatic recognition of high frequency words; find specific information in simple texts; use syntax and context when reading for meaning; distinguish fiction and non-fiction texts and the different purposes for reading them

Curriculum links: Science

Focus phonemes: ur, ir, air, o-e

Fast words: there, you, your, what

Word count: 291

Getting started

- Revisit the *ur*, *ir* and *air* graphemes using flash cards of words from the book, e.g. hurts, hair, air, dirt. Add sound buttons and lines for each phoneme, identifying that in these words, two letters (a digraph) make one sound (phoneme).

- Check that children can hear each phoneme in words with adjacent consonants, e.g. *b-r-ai-n*.

- Look at the front cover and read the title and blurb together. Ask children to suggest how our noses help us. Establish that this is an information book and help children to raise questions about noses that the book may answer.

- Look carefully at the illustration on the back cover. Discuss what this diagram shows.

Reading and responding

- Turn to pp2–3. Read p2 with the children. Ask them to feel their own noses and try to find where their noses are hard and soft. Read p3. Pause at the word *nostrils*. Help children to sound this word out *n-o-s-t-r-i-l-s*, hearing all of the phonemes, and blending them to read.

- Look at the word *nose*. Revise the split digraph pattern *o-e*. Ask children to suggest other words with the *o-e* pattern, e.g. hose, rose.